DISGUSTING & DREADFUL SCIENCE

Slimy Spawn

and other gruesome life cycles

by Barbara Taylor

W

FRANKLIN WATTS

LONDON•SYDNEY

First published in 2014 by Franklin Watts

Copyright © Franklin Watts 2014

Franklin Watts
338 Euston Road
London NW1 3BH

Franklin Watts Australia
Level 17/207 Kent Street, Sydney, NSW 2000

Produced by Penny Worms & Graham Rich, Book Packagers

A CIP catalogue record for this book is available from the British Library.

Dewey Decimal Classification Number: 571.8

ISBN 978 1 4451 3565 6
Library eBook ISBN 978 1 4451 3566 3

Printed in China

Franklin Watts is a division of Hachette Children's Books, an Hachette UK company.

www.hachette.co.uk

Picture credits

Alamy: 10b (E.R.Degginger). **Corbis images:** 8r (D. Parer & E. Parer-Cook/Minden Pictures). **Getty images:** 28r (Mitsuru Sakurai/Stone). **iStockphoto.com:** title page (Dean Murray), eyeball cartoon (Elaine Barker), cover and 19b/spawn (Tree4Two), cover and 10t/bed bug (animatedfunk). **Nature Picture Library:** 10t (Anup Shah). **Shutterstock.com:** cover/mealworms (Michael Wesemann), cover/rat (M.I.ke), cover and 19b/frog (Lightspring), cover/fly (Vinicus Tupinamba), cover/snake (fivespots), cover/spider (Kirsanov Valiriy Vladimirovich), cover/beetle (bluecrayola), 4l (CLIPAREA/Custom media), 4b (Lyudmyla Kharlamova), 5t (Zurijeta), 5c (Eric Isselee), 6t (Swapan Photography), 7t (belizar), 7c (Eric Isselee), 7b (Willyam Bradberry), 8l (worldwildlifewonders), 9r (Eric Isselee), 10b (Trevor Kelly), 11cr (Sarawut Padungkwan), 12cl (elen studio), 12cr (Krasowit), 12b (BlueRingMedia), 13t (Gleb Tarro), 13c (B. Speckart), 13b (ACEgan), 14t (Sphinx Wang), 15r (3drenderings), 15l (Lia Caldes), 16t (Eric Isselee), 16b (GMH Photography), 17c (Dr. Morley Read), 17b (Gentoo Multimedia Limited), 18b (Eric Isselee), 19t (snapgalleria), 19cl (Eric Isselee), 21cl (cerobit), 22tr (RAStudio), 22c (Napat), 22br (smuay), 23t (BlueRingMedia), 23c (Henrik Larsson), 24tr (Olga Guitere), 24cr (Robert Red), 24b (Miles Boyer), 25tr (Tessa Palmer), 25cl (noppharat), 26t (Eric Isselee), 27tr (D. Kucharski K. Kucharska), 27b/mealworm and pupa (D. Kucharski K. Kucharska), 27br (Kletr), 28bl (kurt G.), 29t (Dr Morley Read), 29c (vnlit), 29b (alslutsky). **Wikipedia:** 20b (Tom Oates), 27cr (Dbenzhuser).

All other illustrations by Graham Rich
Every attempt has been made to clear copyright. Should there be any inadvertent omission, please apply to the publisher for rectification.

Contents

Life goes in gruesome cycles

Life cycles can be a truly gruesome business. Most animals, such as humans, have simple life cycles – they start off as eggs, then they hatch or are born (a gooey, messy time) and grow into an adult, ready to make more babies. But some animals have a different pattern to their life cycle – and some go through BIG changes.

DID YOU KNOW?

Different species from the same group of animals may have different life cycles. Most snakes, for example, lay eggs, but some snakes give birth to live young.

Sperm

It takes two...

A human baby begins to develop when a sperm from a man joins with an egg from a woman. Over a period of nine months, this egg develops to form a baby inside a mother's womb. At birth, a human baby is helpless and has to be looked after by its parents.

Egg

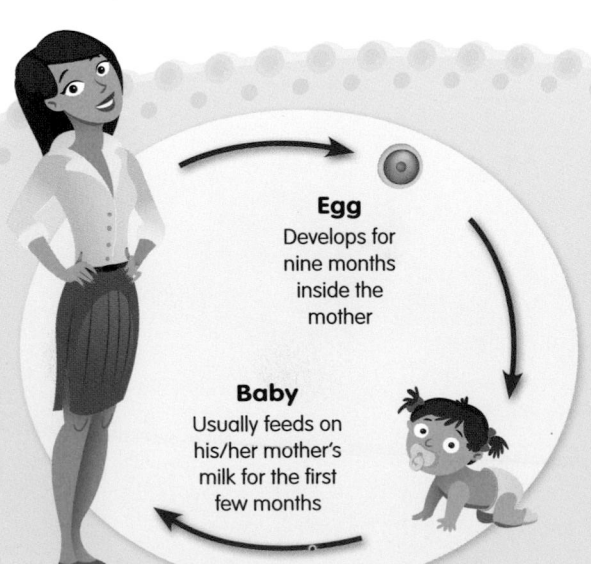

Adult
Fully grown by 17 to 20 years old, and the female is able to have her own babies

Egg
Develops for nine months inside the mother

Baby
Usually feeds on his/her mother's milk for the first few months

Life cycle

A human life cycle has three stages. Humans usually have one baby at a time and spend many years looking after and raising their young.

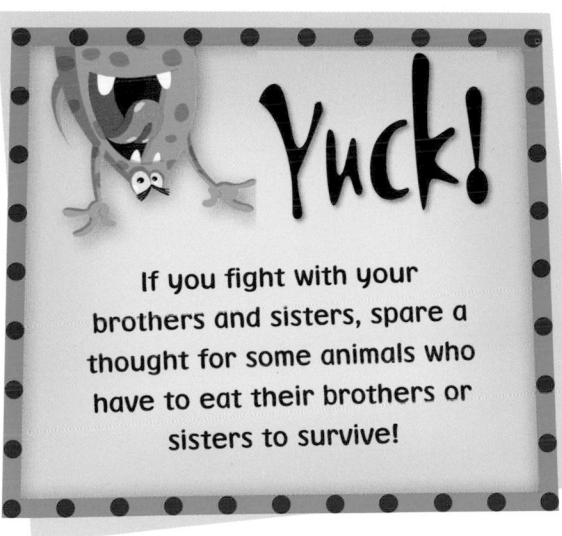

Yuck!

If you fight with your brothers and sisters, spare a thought for some animals who have to eat their brothers or sisters to survive!

Growing...

Babies grow quickly during the first year of their lives. They learn to crawl or walk and say a few words. Growth slows down during childhood, but speeds up again during puberty (11-15 years) when changes happen that make reproduction (producing babies) possible.

Egg

Caterpillar (larva)

Moth (adult)

Pupa

Big changes

Although humans change quite a lot from birth to adulthood, some animals, such as butterflies and moths, change shape completely during their life cycle. This is called metamorphosis. The young may live in different places from the adults or feed on different foods, so they don't compete with their parents. Butterflies and moths have four stages in their life cycle, egg, larva, pupa and adult.

See for Yourself

Raising caterpillars

Try keeping butterfly caterpillars and watch the four stages of their life cycle: egg, caterpillar, pupa and adult. Cover the open end of a cardboard box with gauze or fine mesh. Place the box over a pot containing a food plant, such as nettles. Add the caterpillars and wait for big changes to happen! Don't forget to release the adults into the wild when they emerge.

Life cycles can involve slimy eggs, flesh-eating babies, dreadful parents and disgusting parasites. Turn the page to find out more...

Hairy, scary mammals

Mammals can be horribly hairy creatures, but their babies are often wriggly, squirmy and hairless little things when they are born! Almost all mammal babies develop inside their mother, and she is the only animal mother who produces milk to feed her young. Mammals also protect their babies and teach them to look after themselves.

ZZZZZZZZZZ

Ugly pups

When baby rats are born, they have wrinkly pink skin, their eyes are under the skin on their faces, and their ears are small buds on the sides of the head. Even the fingers and toes are not developed. But after only 21 days, their eyes are open, their ears are sticking out, they have teeth and they have a warm, furry coat. They are ready to "get up and go"!

Life cycle

There are three stages to a rat life cycle. Baby rats grow inside their mother for about 22 days before they are ready to be born. The mother rat gives birth to 6–13 pups. One pup is born every five to ten minutes! The baby rats grow quickly and when they are only five weeks old, they can have babies of their own.

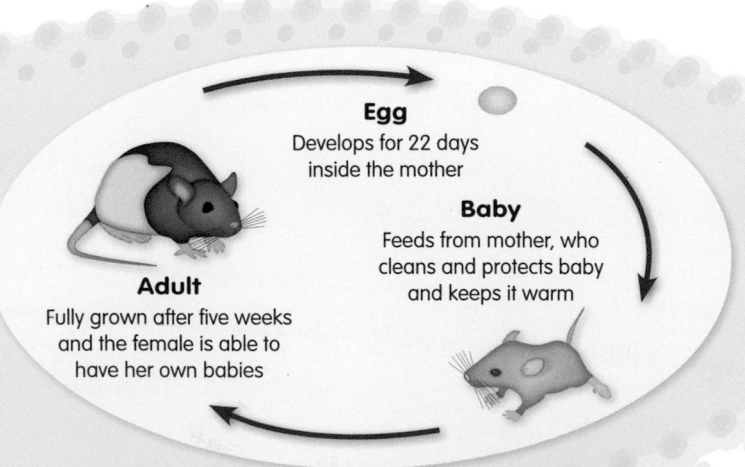

Egg
Develops for 22 days inside the mother

Baby
Feeds from mother, who cleans and protects baby and keeps it warm

Adult
Fully grown after five weeks and the female is able to have her own babies

Yuck!

Naked mole rats have hardly any fur so they are pink and wrinkly all through their lives.

DID YOU KNOW?

Australia's platypus and spiny anteater are two super weird mammals – their babies hatch out of eggs!

Rat milk

Baby rats feed on their mother's milk for up to 18 hours a day! They suckle from teats on their mother's body. Mother rats feed their babies for about four weeks, until they are fully grown. All this feeding drains a lot of the mother's energy. By the time her babies are ready to start exploring on their own, the mother rat is exhausted…

Too many babies!

A female rat may have up to 100 babies in a year!

Mother and baby

Water birth

Like humans, whales and dolphins usually give birth to one or two babies at a time. They are born underwater and the mother has to lift them up to the surface or they could drown! Even though they live in water, dolphins breathe air, just like other mammals.

7

Marsupial madness

Can you imagine a baby small enough to fit onto a teaspoon? Well, that's how tiny some marsupial babies are, such as kangaroos and koalas. Luckily, their mothers have a handy pouch of skin to carry them in until they are fully developed. Marsupials are a special group of mammals that live mostly in Australia or New Guinea but a few live in North and South America.

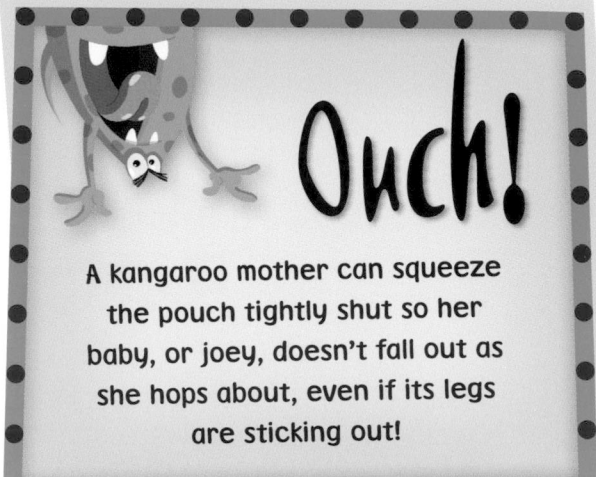

Ouch!

A kangaroo mother can squeeze the pouch tightly shut so her baby, or joey, doesn't fall out as she hops about, even if its legs are sticking out!

Kangaroo with baby in pouch

Jumping jelly babies

Even though marsupial babies look fragile, they have strong front legs to crawl from the birth opening up to a pouch on their mother's belly all by themselves! They can't see where they are going. They just follow the smell of her milk. Once in the pouch, they hold on tightly to a teat and drink milk to help them grow and develop.

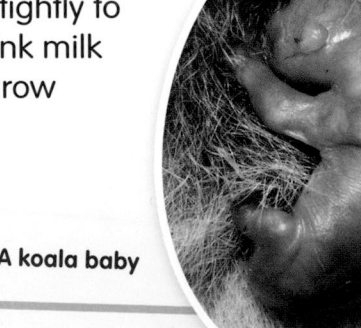

A koala baby

8

Life cycle

A baby koala stays safe and warm in its mother's pouch for the first six months of its life. When it is ready to leave the pouch, the baby koala leans out to lick some of its mother's watery poo, called pap. Bacteria in this pap helps the young koalas to digest the tough gum tree leaves it eats outside the pouch.

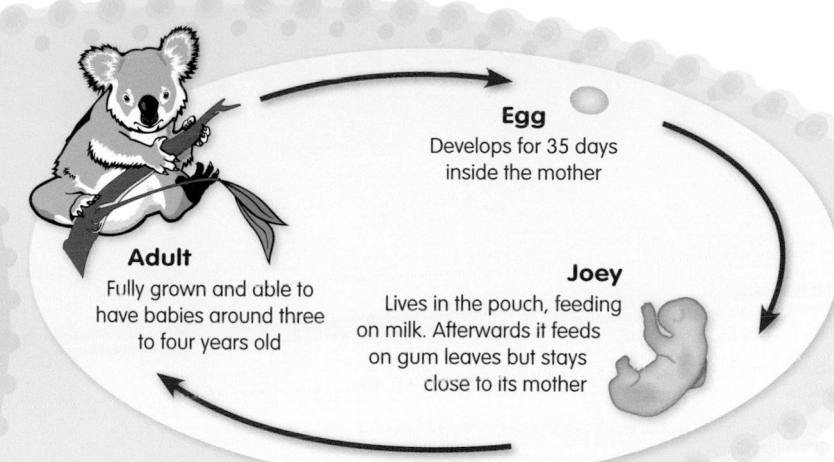

Adult
Fully grown and able to have babies around three to four years old

Egg
Develops for 35 days inside the mother

Joey
Lives in the pouch, feeding on milk. Afterwards it feeds on gum leaves but stays close to its mother

Climb aboard

Kangaroos and koalas have just one joey at a time, while other marsupials, such as opossums, have several. After the joeys leave the pouch, the mothers still look after them and carry them around. Koalas get piggybacks, but a kangaroo joey will jump into its mother's pouch if it's frightened or wants a drink, even if she has a newborn.

DID YOU KNOW?

At birth, 20 Virginia opossum babies would fit onto a teaspoon!

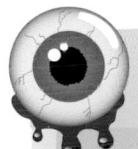

See for Yourself

The teat test

Pour some yoghurt into the fingers of a rubber glove and see how they grow fatter. This is what happens inside a baby marsupial's mouth as it sucks milk from its mother's teat. The teat swells and becomes so fat that the baby can't pull away. It is "stuck" there, safe from harm as the mother moves around. As the baby grows, its jaws get bigger and it is able to pull its mouth off the teat.

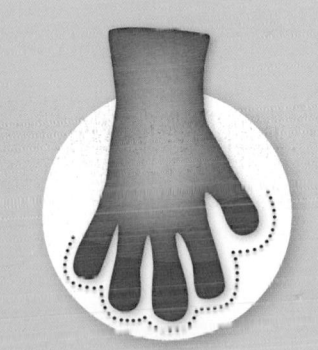

Fierce reptiles

Have you ever wondered where dinosaurs came from? Surprisingly, they all hatched out of eggs, even the big fierce dinosaurs, such as Tyrannosaurus rex! Most dinosaurs were reptiles and most of their modern relatives, such as birds, crocodiles, snakes and lizards, still hatch out of eggs today. A few snakes and lizards give birth to tiny babies instead of laying eggs.

Don't mess with mother

A mother crocodile will attack any predator that comes too close to her eggs during hatching time. The mother also gulps her newly hatched babies into her mouth... but she doesn't eat them! Instead, she carries them down to water and guards them to keep them safe while they snap up insects and tadpoles with their sharp teeth.

Horrible hatchlings

Baby reptiles push their way out of their eggs using a sharp piece of skin called an egg tooth on their snout. Sometimes mum helps.

DID YOU KNOW?

Female sea turtles dig deep holes for their eggs on sandy beaches. Their eggs are soft and flexible, so there is less chance of them cracking when they drop into the sandy hole. Many sea turtles lay more than 100 eggs at a time. A hawksbill sea turtle once laid 258 eggs in one go!

Life cycle

There are three stages to a crocodile life cycle. The baby crocodile spends two to three months developing inside its waterproof egg. It feeds on the egg yolk and breathes air through the shell. When it hatches out, the baby croc looks like its parents and can look after itself straight away. It has very sharp teeth!

Egg
Hatches in two to three months

Baby crocodile
Grows about 30 cm each year

Adult
After 10 to 15 years, a crocodile is fully grown and the female can have babies of her own

Yikes!

Tree snakes often give birth to live young, high up in trees. The baby snakes are born with clear, sticky bags around them. The bags stick to the tree's branches and stop the babies from falling down to the ground.

Dinosaur eggs

Millions of years ago, dinosaurs laid eggs with hard shells, just like birds do today – fossils of dinosaur nests prove this! Some even guarded their nests and looked after their young – predators would have thought twice before arguing with a dinosaur mum…

Live births

Some lizards, such as the common lizard, and snakes, including boas, rattlesnakes and adders, give birth to babies. Keeping babies inside the mother's body helps keep the babies warm in cold places. The weight of the babies, however, makes it hard for the mother to move quickly.

This baby copperhead snake has just been born.

A fishy tragedy

Fish are among the worst parents in the world. Most fish lay lots of very small eggs and swim off, leaving their babies to fend for themselves. Needless to say, few survive. But salmon go to extraordinary lengths for their babies, journeying thousands of kilometres to lay their eggs in the perfect place. And after laying their eggs, some types of salmon die.

Salmon use their strong muscles to make mighty leaps up waterfalls.

Going home

Salmon are born in freshwater but live most of their lives in the sea, where there is more food for them to eat. They return to the river where they hatched to lay their own eggs, finding their birth river by the smell of the water. The females then lay thousands of round, red eggs in a gravel nest called a redd.

The bodies of the young salmon have to change before they can survive in salty sea water – without this "smolting" process, their bodies would explode in the sea!

Life cycle

There are five stages to a salmon life cycle. The eggs hatch after around two to three months, depending on the water temperature. The newly hatched alevin (babies) stay in the nest and feed from a yolk sac attached to their bodies until they are bigger.

Alevin
Stays in the nest for two to three weeks

Parr
The young fish is camouflaged and leaves the nest to find food

Smolt
The silver smolt swims towards the sea, adapting to salt water

Egg
Hatches in two to three months

Adult
The male turns red and develops a hooked jaw. Females are ready to lay eggs after two years.

Super survivors

Baby salmon have a dreadful survival rate. They are a perfect food for many predators, including larger fish and birds, such as herons and kingfishers. Out of every 8,000 eggs, only 50 smolt survive and only two of these survive to become adults. Bears catch a lot of adult salmon as they leap up waterfalls so even the adult salmon may not complete their life cycle.

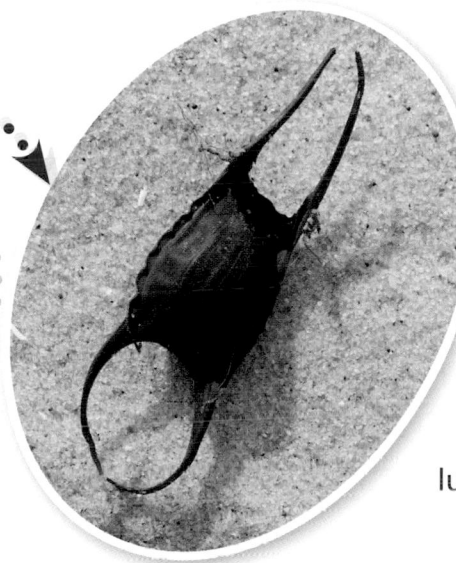

Shark eggs are protected inside strong, leathery cases. Empty egg cases are known as "mermaid's purses".

Sharks

Sharks are fish, too, but only about one third of all shark species lay eggs. The rest give birth to live pups. Some mums have only one or two pups, others have over 100. Shark pups swim away from their mothers as soon as they are born, as she might be hungry enough to eat them! They then have to fend for themselves – luckily they have a full set of sharp teeth!

Yuck!

Male jawfish hold their eggs inside their big mouths for warmth and protection. When the eggs hatch, the male spits out the tiny baby fish and they swim away.

shape-shifting crustaceans

Boxer crabs are also called pom-pom crabs because they carry stinging sea anemones in their claws for defence.

From crabs and shrimps to barnacles and woodlice, most crusty crustaceans hatch out of their eggs looking more like aliens than their parents. They start life as tiny, see-through floating larvae, which change shape completely as they grow up. To grow bigger, the larvae have to shed, or moult, their outer skin and grow a bigger one.

Mother crab

A female crab carries a mass of eggs under her body (this boxer crab has orange eggs). The eggs are attached to fine hairs on her body so they don't fall off. They are well protected from harm and predators while they develop.

DID YOU KNOW?

A female blue crab can lay up to two million eggs at a time, but only one out of every million eggs survives to become an adult crab.

Life cycle

There are four main stages to a shore crab's life cycle. The zoea larva has a tail for swimming and spikes for protection. The megalopa larva settles on the sea floor and changes into a baby crab.

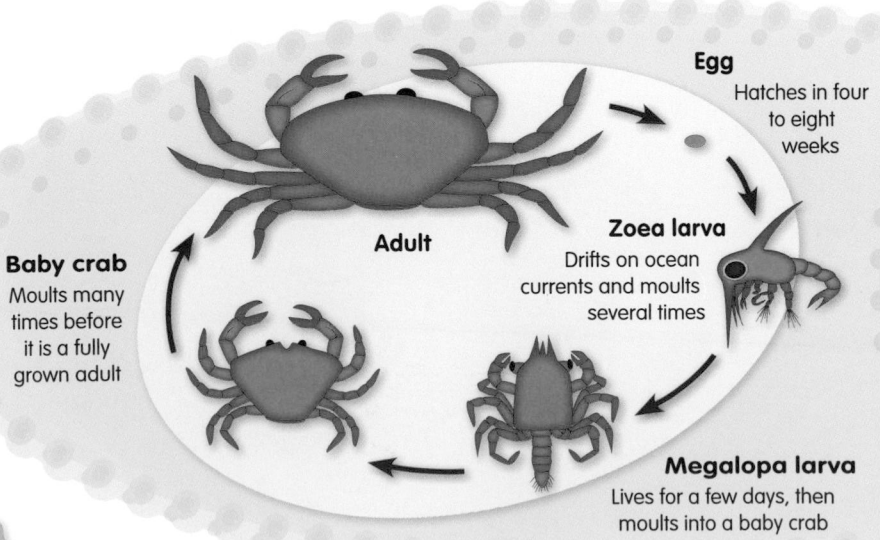

Egg
Hatches in four to eight weeks

Zoea larva
Drifts on ocean currents and moults several times

Adult

Baby crab
Moults many times before it is a fully grown adult

Megalopa larva
Lives for a few days, then moults into a baby crab

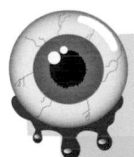

Watching woodlice

Woodlice are crustaceans too. They like to live in damp places because their skin is not waterproof. To watch them closely, put some upside-down flower pots among a pile of logs, twigs, dead leaves or bark and wait for them to move in!

Whale food

Tiny crustaceans and their larvae drift in the ocean and most of them are eaten by much larger animals, such as whales and penguins. Blue whales need to eat about 40 million crustaceans called krill every day!

Krill are tiny crustaceans that look like shrimp.

It's not easy being me.

Barnacles

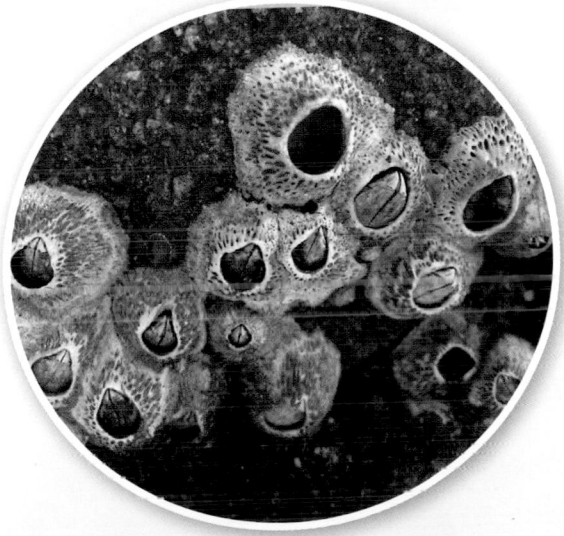

Barnacles start life as tiny larvae that drift through the sea before gluing themselves to a rock and changing into an adult. They stay fixed to the rock for up to five years, standing on their head inside a hard case and using their "legs" to grab food from the water.

Ouch!

Adult barnacles can dig down deep into whale skin, forming a sharp suit of armour. Humpback whales have been found with almost 450 kg of barnacles living on their skin!

Big bully birds

A bird's life cycle starts inside an egg with a hard shell. Female birds lay eggs because they would be too heavy to fly with babies inside them. After the chicks hatch, parent birds work hard to feed and protect them and keep them warm.

But while bird parents are protective, some chicks, such as owls, can be badly bullied by their big brothers and sisters, especially if there is not enough food to go round.

Mother barn owls sit on their eggs to keep them warm for about nine weeks.

Helpless!

Owls are blind, naked and helpless when they hatch out. They can also take several hours to escape from their shells and the process is so tiring that many babies die of exhaustion.

Owl babies

Owl babies look cute with all those fluffy feathers but they can be really mean! Female barn owls lay one egg every two or three days for two weeks, rather than laying all their eggs at once. But because the owlets hatch out at different times, the older, bigger owlets may take all the food and the smallest ones may starve. Sometimes, the big bully owlets even eat their dead brothers and sisters.

Baby barn owls

Life cycle

There are three stages to every bird's life cycle. A baby bird chips its way out of the egg using a pointed egg tooth on top of its bill. It grows fluffy down feathers to keep warm, as well as body feathers. It is only able to feed itself when it grows its adult feathers.

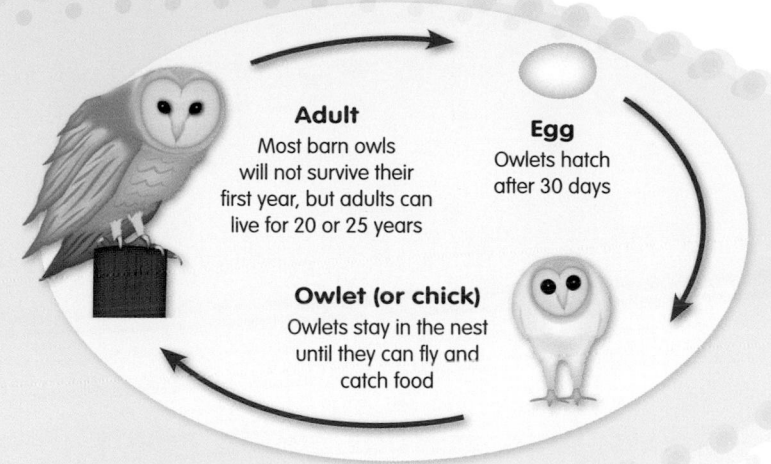

Adult
Most barn owls will not survive their first year, but adults can live for 20 or 25 years

Egg
Owlets hatch after 30 days

Owlet (or chick)
Owlets stay in the nest until they can fly and catch food

Smelly nappies

Barn owls usually lay their eggs on a mat of broken and squashed pellets, which are the hair and bones of small animals that the owls spit out. This smelly mat is ideal for soaking up all the wee and poo, just like nappies! Hold your nose if you're near a nest though…

Yuck!

At two weeks old, owlets can eat whole mice or voles, although it may take a while to swallow a meal!

Papa penguins

Emperor penguins lay only one egg. The male holds the egg on his feet and keeps it warm all through the winter. By the time the mother returns from the sea to look after her newly hatched chick, the male has lost half his weight.

slimy amphibian spawn

Amphibians, such as frogs, toads, newts and salamanders, lead a double life. Most of them can live on both land and in water, although they usually lay their slimy, jelly-coated eggs in water. This "spawn" hatches quickly into swimming larvae, which go through a series of big changes, called metamorphosis, before turning into adults.

Only five out of 100 eggs, tadpoles or young amphibians that hatch each year make it to adulthood. The rest are eaten by predators, such as fish, snakes, birds, foxes or other tadpoles!

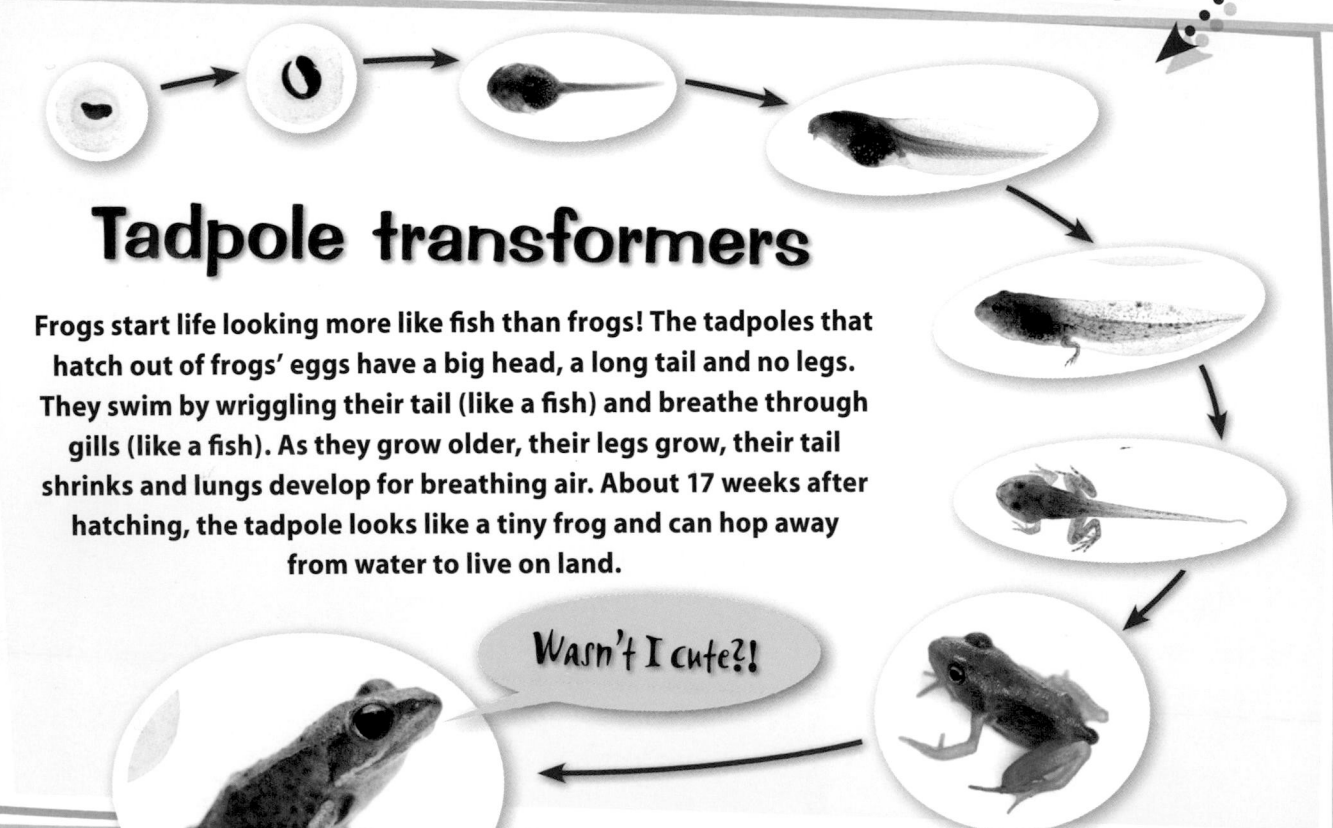

Tadpole transformers

Frogs start life looking more like fish than frogs! The tadpoles that hatch out of frogs' eggs have a big head, a long tail and no legs. They swim by wriggling their tail (like a fish) and breathe through gills (like a fish). As they grow older, their legs grow, their tail shrinks and lungs develop for breathing air. About 17 weeks after hatching, the tadpole looks like a tiny frog and can hop away from water to live on land.

Wasn't I cute?!

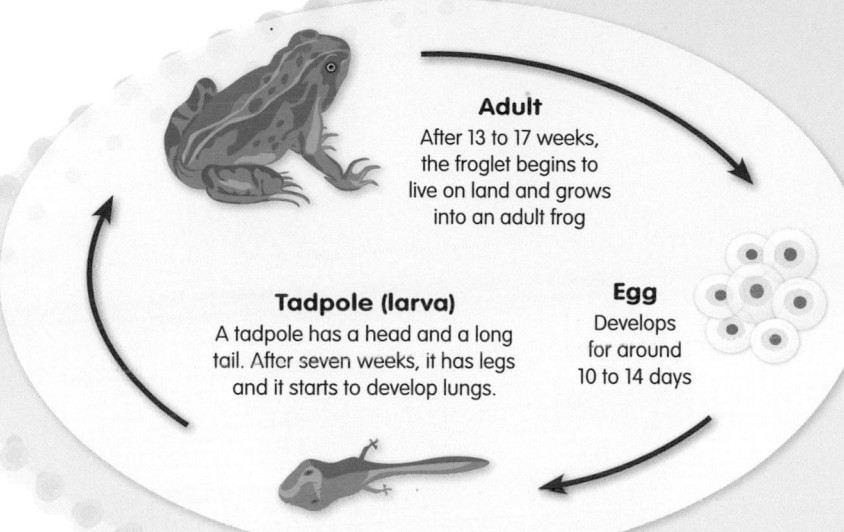

Adult
After 13 to 17 weeks, the froglet begins to live on land and grows into an adult frog

Tadpole (larva)
A tadpole has a head and a long tail. After seven weeks, it has legs and it starts to develop lungs.

Egg
Develops for around 10 to 14 days

Life cycle

There are three main stages to a frog's life cycle. Frogs usually live in the water as tadpoles and then spend some or almost all of their adult lives on land. Tadpoles are mostly vegetarian, but they become meat-eaters as soon as they are froglets, living on land.

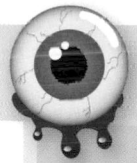

DID YOU KNOW?

A few amphibians, such as fire salamanders, give birth to babies instead of laying eggs. They look like tiny adults, but have gills for breathing oxygen from the water. Eventually they develop lungs for breathing air and start living on land.

Sticky spawn

Amphibian eggs don't have a hard shell, like bird or reptile eggs. The jelly around the black eggs stops them from drying out and keeps them warm. It also protects the eggs from predators, who don't like eating the sticky, slimy jelly! Frogs lay eggs glued together in clumps, while toads lay eggs in long chains, like strings of pearls. Newts wrap their eggs individually in water plants to keep them safe.

See for Yourself

Collecting spawn

It's fascinating to collect tadpoles and watch them changing into adults. Make sure you have 3 to 5 tadpoles per litre of pond water, and have some rocks and plants for the tiny froglets to climb out of the water. It's really important for the delicate balance of nature that you return the froglets to the same pond or river that you collected them from.

Itchy, scratchy insects

Insects are small, six-legged animals, which usually hatch out of eggs. Some insects, such as bed bugs or earwigs, look like tiny adults when they hatch and just grow bigger. They are called nymphs, and have a strong, protective skin, called an exoskeleton. The exoskeleton cannot stretch. So as the young nymphs grow, they have to shed, or moult, their old exoskeleton to grow a bigger one.

The proboscis is like a sharp straw that the bed bug uses to stab its victim. But it's nearly painless – you only know you've been bitten when the bites itch.

An adult bed bug is good at scuttling around on its six long legs, but it can't jump or fly. Its feeding tube, or proboscis, is made up of two hollow tubes. One tube injects spit, or saliva, to keep a sleeping person's blood flowing, while the other tube sucks up the blood.

Caring parents

Very few insects look after their eggs. Female earwigs are an interesting exception. They guard their eggs for months until they hatch, even licking them to keep them clean! When the eggs hatch into nymphs, the mother earwig feeds them until they are big enough to leave the nest.

Life cycle

Bed bugs have a three-stage life cycle – egg, nymph, adult. The nymphs moult five times before reaching their adult size. They feed once during each of these stages, which last about a week. Adults usually feed every five to ten days but can live for up to 18 months without feeding!

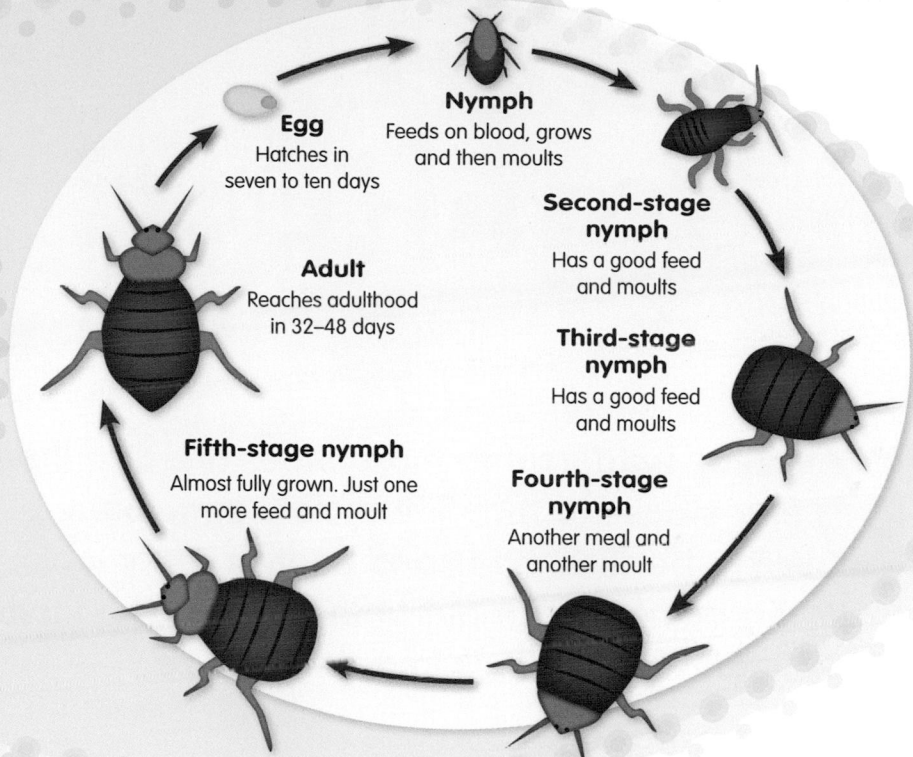

Egg
Hatches in seven to ten days

Nymph
Feeds on blood, grows and then moults

Second-stage nymph
Has a good feed and moults

Third-stage nymph
Has a good feed and moults

Fourth-stage nymph
Another meal and another moult

Fifth-stage nymph
Almost fully grown. Just one more feed and moult

Adult
Reaches adulthood in 32–48 days

DEAD Gross!

This messy mixture is the shed exoskeletons of nymphs and newly laid eggs. However, the nymphs are no bigger than a pinhead and the eggs are as small as a speck of dust. No wonder bed bugs are hard to find! These stubborn, clever critters are really hard to get rid of, especially since they usually come out at night.

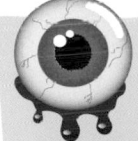

See for Yourself

Multiplying maths

Female bed bugs can lay five eggs a day and the eggs can hatch in seven days. If you brought one female and one male, let's call them Beth and Bob, into your home and Beth laid five eggs a day, you could have seven bed bugs a week later (Beth, Bob and five first-stage nymphs) plus 35 eggs. If Beth continues to lay five eggs a day, how many could you have in 14 days?

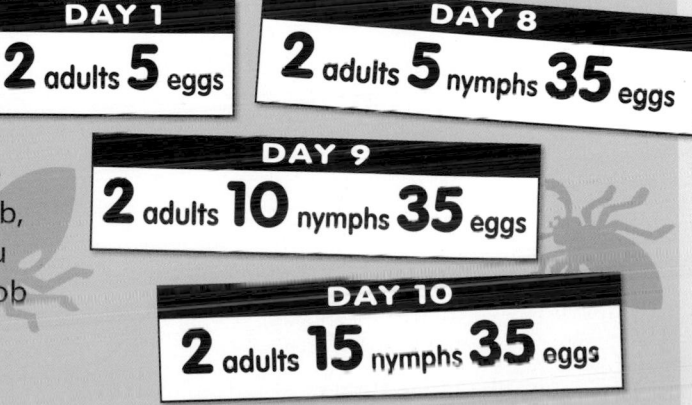

DAY 1
2 adults 5 eggs

DAY 8
2 adults 5 nymphs 35 eggs

DAY 9
2 adults 10 nymphs 35 eggs

DAY 10
2 adults 15 nymphs 35 eggs

In 14 days, you'd have 37 bed bugs in your bed (Beth, Bob and 35 nymphs) plus 35 eggs.

Beware mosquitoes!

Buzzing, bothersome mosquitoes are also insects but they have four stages to their life cycle – egg, larva, pupa and adult – just like butterflies, bees and beetles. They look very different from the adults when they hatch out of their eggs. The larva then has to moult its exoskeleton several times in order to grow.

The larvae feed on algae and small water animals.

Lazy larva

Mosquito eggs float on the water and hatch into legless, worm-like larvae, also known as "wrigglers"! The larvae are the feeding stage of the life cycle and have to breathe air from the surface. Most of them have a tube for breathing at the end of their bodies and they hang down from the water's surface.

Magic change

The pupa floats head upwards at the water's surface.

When they are fully grown, the larvae turn into a resting stage, called a pupa. Inside the pupa, the body of the larva is broken down and rebuilt into an adult mosquito with wings. This only takes a few days. Then the pupa's exoskeleton splits and the adult mosquito climbs out.

Life cycle

Mosquitoes lay their eggs in water and their larvae and pupae live in water. Adult mosquitoes however, live in the air. Adult males live only a week, while females live for six to eight weeks.

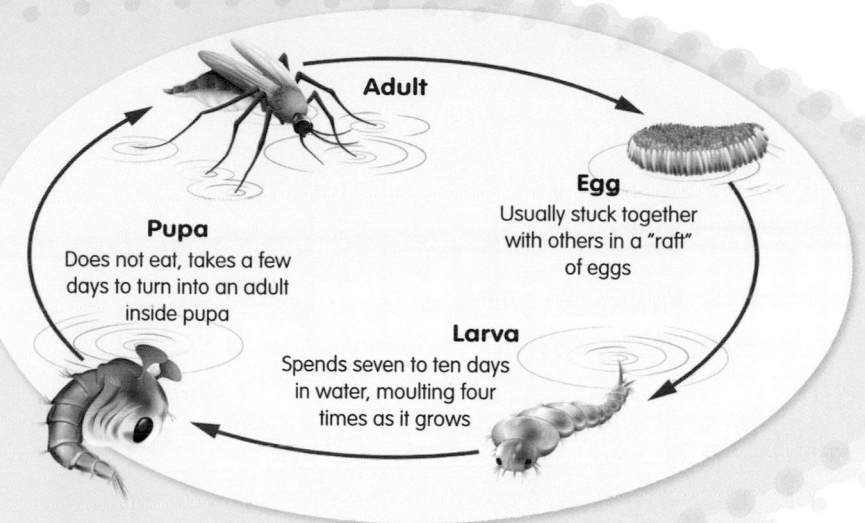

Adult

Egg
Usually stuck together with others in a "raft" of eggs

Pupa
Does not eat, takes a few days to turn into an adult inside pupa

Larva
Spends seven to ten days in water, moulting four times as it grows

Beware!

If you've been bitten by a mosquito, it was a female! Male mosquitoes feed on plants but most females have to feed on blood or their eggs will not develop. They bite using a sharp, pointed feeding tube, which injects chemicals to keep the blood flowing and reduce pain. It's these chemicals that make mosquito bites itch.

Yuck!

Scientists have discovered two things that attract mosquitoes – stinky feet and a type of cheese that smells like stinky feet! The cheese is called Limberger, so watch out if you have a Limberger sandwich.

A female mosquito can drink up to three times her weight of blood at one meal! Her abdomen swells as it fills with the red blood. Then she rests for a few days before laying up to 300 eggs at a time.

Spiders galore

Just one spider makes some people shudder and scream, but some giant spiders have over 1,000 babies at a time. Now that's the stuff of nightmares! Fortunately, baby spiders are very small and have no hairs, spines, claws or venom until they shed their exoskeleton for the first time. Most baby spiders fend for themselves, but some mother spiders guard and feed their young.

Egg carrier

Mother spiders protect their eggs inside a silk sac or cocoon, which may be fixed to plants or hidden under leaves or rocks. Many mother spiders carry their egg sacs around with them. They often sunbathe, as the heat speeds up the development of the baby spiders!

Klingons

Baby wolf spiders ride piggyback on their mother's back, clinging on to her hairs. The mother always trails safety lines of silk behind her, so if the babies fall off, they can easily climb back on board.

Nursery tent

When her eggs are ready to hatch, the female nursery-web spider builds a silk tent for her egg case. She stands guard over the eggs and baby spiders for a week or so, until the baby spiders leave the tent to start a life of their own.

Moulting...

Spiders are not insects – they are arachnids – but they still have exoskeletons and have to moult in order to grow. Each moult takes a few hours, and it is a dangerous time for spiders. They could damage their legs as they wriggle free, and they are vulnerable to predators.

That's better!

Yuck!

Some mother spiders die before their babies leave home and so the young spiders feed on their own mother's body!

Life cycle

A spider has three stages to its life cycle. Most spider eggs hatch within a few days or weeks. The baby spiders moult five to ten times as they grow into adults. Then they often produce a long strand of silk and float away on a warm breeze.

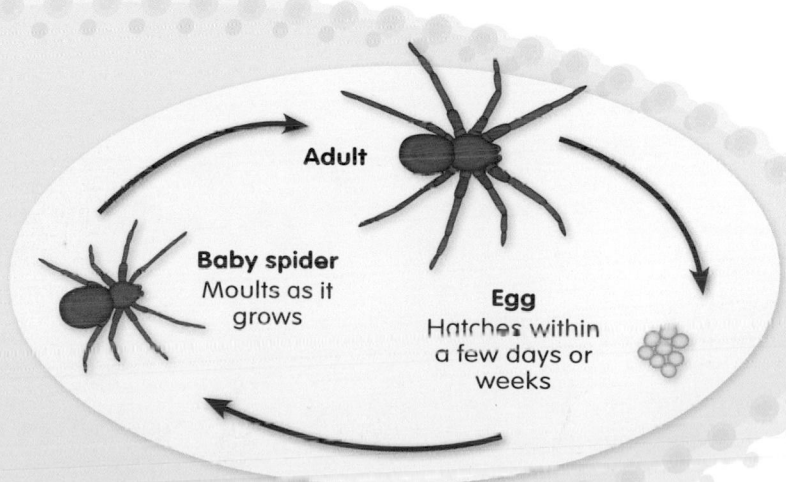

Adult

Baby spider
Moults as it grows

Egg
Hatches within a few days or weeks

Revolting worms

I don't like the sound of that!

Wriggly, squishy and downright disgusting, worms are not most people's favourite animals. Some are particularly revolting because they live inside other animals, including humans! These pesky parasites, such as hairworms, roundworms and tapeworms, are like stowaways on ships – they sneak on board, steal food and make themselves comfortable. When they reproduce, most parasitic worms find a different host for their babies. Eeww!

Thanks a million

Some horses may have as many as a million small redworms living inside their gut! Large redworms are much more dangerous however. The adults eat the lining of the gut wall and the larvae get into the bloodstream, so they can travel around the horse's body. The damage they cause inside the horse can kill it.

Life cycle

A roundworm has three stages to its life cycle. Worm eggs pass out of the host animal in its poo. Larvae hatch out of the eggs. These are eaten by insects, mice or birds, which in turn are eaten by animals and the life cycle begins again.

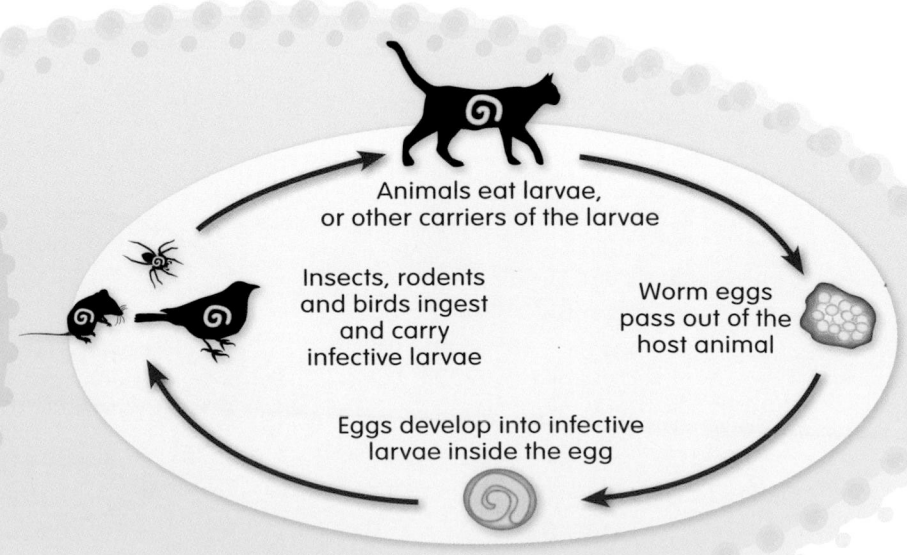

Animals eat larvae, or other carriers of the larvae

Insects, rodents and birds ingest and carry infective larvae

Worm eggs pass out of the host animal

Eggs develop into infective larvae inside the egg

26

Ouch!

When puppies or kittens drink their mother's milk, they may also take in the larvae of roundworms. These roundworms set up home in their gut. Female roundworms can produce 200,000 eggs in a day!

Snail take-over

This snail seems to have a caterpillar growing out of its head! In fact, this "caterpillar" is a part of the snail's body, which is now full of flatworm larvae! When a caterpillar-loving bird eats the larvae, they develop into adults inside the bird. The bird passes out flatworm eggs in its droppings, which are eaten by snails and the life cycle continues.

Body snatchers

Grasshoppers and crickets sometimes drink in the larvae of hairworms, which develop into adult worms inside their bodies. It is not known how, but the worms make their hosts throw themselves into water, where the worms produce eggs. Unfortunately, grasshoppers and crickets can't swim!

You can see the hairworm crawling out of the rear of this katydid cricket!

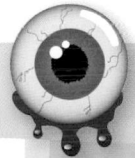

See for Yourself

From worm to beetle

A mealworm is the larva of the darkling beetle. Buy some small mealworms from a pet shop and keep them in a clear container covered with tin foil. Keep the foil in place with an elastic band and make small holes in the foil. Feed the mealworms with bran flakes, oatmeal and small pieces of carrot. Over a few weeks, watch as the mealworm changes into a pupa and eventually into an adult beetle. This makes a tasty meal for a wild bird.

Mealworm

Pupa

Adult beetle

Eaten alive!

And finally the most disgusting and dreadful life cycles of all! These involve eating other animals alive! And there are plenty of gruesome examples. Many insects lay their eggs on or in other creatures so their larvae have plenty of fresh, living food right in front of them when they hatch out.

Wicked wasp

Female tarantula hawk wasps are a tarantula spider's worst nightmare. When she finds a tarantula in its burrow, the wasp stings it with just enough venom to paralyse the spider (stop it moving). Then she drags the spider to her own burrow and lays an egg on its body. The egg hatches into a larva, which chews its way into the living spider and feeds on its flesh. When the larva turns into an adult, it tears itself free of the spider's empty body and flies away. Nice!

This giant wasp grows up to 50 mm long.

Life cycle

There are four stages to a tarantula hawk wasp's life cycle. The female wasp lays only one egg on the spider. The larva feeds on the spider's living body for about 30 days. Then it turns into a pupa and then a wasp.

Egg
Hatches on the spider's body

Adult
The wasp digs its way out and flies away

Larva
Feeds on the spider's body

Pupa
Inside the pupa, the larva changes into a wasp

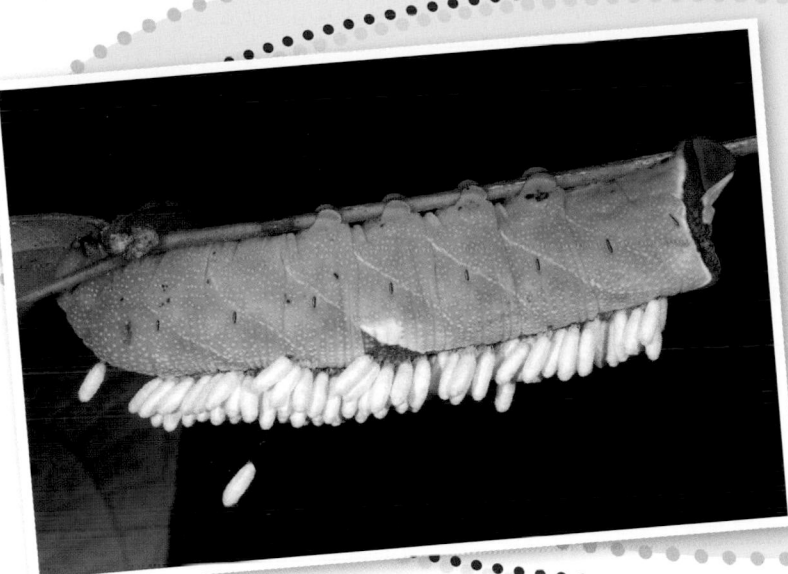

Dead hungry

The white "eggs" hanging from this caterpillar are actually rows of pupae belonging to a wasp. The wasp larvae have already eaten the insides of the caterpillar and are now turning into adults.

Cricket corpse

A female Larra wasp stings a mole cricket to keep it still for a few minutes. Then it lays an egg on the cricket's body, near its legs. The mole cricket soon recovers and burrows back underground, but it is carrying a deadly cargo. The egg hatches into a wasp larva, which feeds on the mole cricket's body, eventually killing it. Then the larva turns into a pupa on the cricket's dead body.

Mole cricket

Adult Larra wasp

You won't feel a thing...

Yuck!

Caterpillars of the cabbage white butterfly are sometimes attacked by tiny flies, which lay their eggs inside the caterpillars. The grubs that hatch out of the eggs eat the caterpillars alive from the inside out...

So you see, all living things have a life cycle. Some are simple. Some are tough. And some are gruesome! But no species would be here on the planet without one.

Glossary

abdomen the back part of an insect's body

algae simple, plant-like living things that usually make their own food

amphibian an animal, such as a frog, that lives partly in water and partly on land

bacteria microscopic, one-celled living things

cocoon a silk covering or case made by caterpillars when they turn into a pupa

crustacean a small animal, such as a crab, with a hard, crusty shell, that usually lives in water

exoskeleton the hard outer shell or casing of an insect or spider

gills body parts used by some animals to breathe underwater

larva (plural **larvae**) the immature stage in the life cycle of certain animals, such as insects

life cycle the pattern of changes that takes place from the beginning to the end of an animal's life

mammal an intelligent, hairy animal that feeds its young on mother's milk

marsupials a mammal, such as a koala, whose young develop inside the mother's pouch

metamorphosis when an animal's body goes through a major change

moulting shedding old skin as an animal grows

nymph the young stage in the life cycle of insects that do not turn into a pupa

parasites living things that live on or inside the body of another living thing

predator an animal that kills and eats other animals, called its prey

proboscis a long, straw-like mouthpart, used for feeding

pupa (plural **pupae**) a resting stage in the life cycle of some insects, during which they change into adults inside a protective case

reptile animals, such as snakes and crocodiles, with dry, scaly skin, who usually lay eggs but some give birth to live young

sperm a cell produced by a male animal to join with a female's egg to form a new animal

tadpole the immature form of a frog or a toad

venom the poison in the bite or sting of some animals, such as spiders

womb a part of the female body in which an egg grows into a baby

Websites and Places to visit

http://ypte.org.uk/animal/amphibians-frogs-toads-and-newts/42
Website of the Young People's Trust for the Environment, with all sorts of amphibian facts and how to make a wildlife pond.

Natural History Museum
Cromwell Road, London, SW7 5BD, UK
Discover sensational butterflies and other creepy crawlies, both online and at the museum.
www.nhm.ac.uk/kids-only/index.html

Oxford University Museum of Natural History, Parks Road, Oxford, OX1 3PW, UK
Check out the reproduction and growth pages in the learning zone.
www.oum.ox.ac.uk

Smithsonian National Museum of Natural History, 10th St & Constitution Ave. NW, Washington D.C. 20560, USA
Live insect zoo and tarantula feedings!
www.mnh.si.edu/index.htm

Australian Museum
6 College Street, Sydney, NSW2010, Australia
Find out about marsupials, tarantulas, the biology of birds and insect life cycles.
australianmuseum.net.au/animals

Monterey Bay Aquarium
886 Cannery Row, Monterey, CA 93940, USA
Information about the life cycles of a range of sea creatures, from barnacles and penguins to sea otters and seahorses.
www.montereybayaquarium.org

National Geographic
Amazing photos of animal babies and hatching eggs as well as all sorts of facts about the life cycles of different animal groups.
www.nationalgeographic.com/animals & kids.nationalgeographic.com/kids

Or check out a zoo near you. Zoos have to know all about animal life cycles because they breed rare and endangered animals and re-introduce them back into the wild.

Index